TO:

_____

FROM:

_____

DATE:

_____

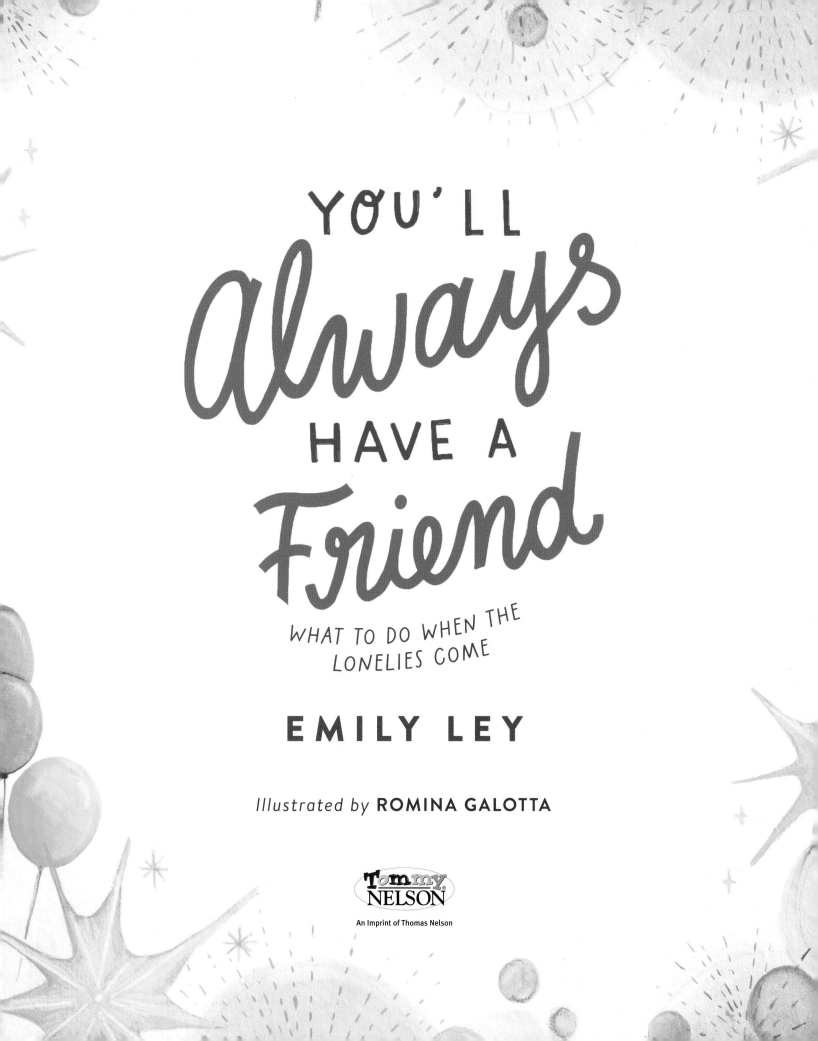

YOU'LL Always HAVE A Friend

WHAT TO DO WHEN THE LONELIES COME

EMILY LEY

Illustrated by **ROMINA GALOTTA**

Tommy NELSON®

An Imprint of Thomas Nelson

You'll Always Have a Friend

© 2024 Emily Ley

Tommy Nelson, PO Box 141000, Nashville, TN 37214

Published in Nashville, Tennessee, by Tommy Nelson. Tommy Nelson is an imprint of Thomas Nelson. Thomas Nelson is a registered trademark of HarperCollins Christian Publishing, Inc.

Published in association with Folio Literary Management LLC, 630 Ninth Avenue, Suite 1101, New York, New York 10036.

Tommy Nelson titles may be purchased in bulk for educational, business, fund-raising, or sales promotional use. For information, please email SpecialMarkets@ThomasNelson.com.

ISBN 978-1-4002-4858-2 (eBook)
ISBN 978-1-4002-4857-5 (HC)

Library of Congress Cataloging-in-Publication Data

Names: Ley, Emily, author. | Galotta, Romina, illustrator.
Title: You'll always have a friend : what to do when the lonelies come / Emily Ley ; illustrated by Romina Galotta.
Description: Nashville, Tennessee : Thomas Nelson, [2024] | Audience: Ages 4-8 | Summary: "Imagine a world where you always have a place at the table, where you always have a friend. This reassuring and empowering book from Emily Ley helps kids realize that they can always have a place, and offers them practical tools to give them confidence and help them overcome lonely times"-- Provided by publisher.
Identifiers: LCCN 2023054289 (print) | LCCN 2023054290 (ebook) | ISBN 9781400248575 (hardcover) | ISBN 9781400248582 (epub)
Subjects: LCSH: Friendship in children--Juvenile literature. | Friendship--Juvenile literature. | Loneliness in children--Juvenile literature. | Loneliness--Juvenile literature.
Classification: LCC HQ784.F7 L49 2024 (print) | LCC HQ784.F7 (ebook) | DDC 302.34083--dc23/eng/20231201
LC record available at https://lccn.loc.gov/2023054289
LC ebook record available at https://lccn.loc.gov/2023054290

Written by Emily Ley
Illustrated by Romina Galotta

Printed in Malaysia

24 25 26 27 28 IMG 6 5 4 3 2 1

Mfr: IMG / Selangor, Malaysia / May 2024 / PO #12232768

To Kennedy.

May you find a friend and be a friend

everywhere you go.

I have important questions.
Some things I'd like to know.
Have you felt the LONELIES lately
or maybe long ago?

Have you ever wondered
while playing **ALL ALONE**
if the other kids could see you
as you got by on your own?

Have you ever felt **LEFT OUT**
or lonely through and through?
Have you ever wished for just one FRIEND
who'd love to play with you?

Has lunchtime ever found you
standing with your tray,
looking to each table
for a friend to **STOP** and SAY . . .

"Hey, we'd love to have you!

Sit here. We'll all make space.

We think you're **REALLY AWESOME**.

You'll always have a place."

Well, I am here to tell you that
you're not the only one.
We all have **WISHED** and HOPED to be
included in the fun.

There are many ways to bring
these lonelies to an end.
Try these tips, and soon you'll find
you'll ALWAYS have a friend.

Treat everyone with kindness.
Be genuine and true.
Anyone would be **LUCKY**
to have a friend like you.

Gather up your confidence.

Walk up and say HELLO.

Smile and wave and share your name.

Let your **BIG HEART** show!

It's okay if you feel nervous.
That's part of how it goes.
You'll plant a little "hello" seed,
and that's how **FRIENDSHIP** grows.

You know what else can be fun?
To be part of a TEAM!
There's something really special
about sharing the same dream.

You don't have to be an all-star
to sign up for something new.
All it takes is a "want to try"
while being BRAVELY you.

Other friends to look for,
who are loyal in every way,
are the sweetest PETS and ANIMALS,
always ready to play!

These cuddly friends are fuzzy,
fluffy, soft, and furry,
always there, right by your side,
to TAKE AWAY your worry.

But if trying to make friends
ever feels too hard to do,
talk with a trusted grown-up
who can help **ENCOURAGE** you.

They may not be your age.
They may not be your size.
But they'll always fill your heart right up
with words so very **WISE**.

Some friends pop up in places
you never thought to look!
You might find brand-new buddies
in the pages of a **BOOK**.

There may be knights and princesses
or dragons to discover.
You can join in their ADVENTURES
by reading from cover to cover.

Still, there's one important friend
who needs your **EXTRA** care.
Guess what? That very friend is YOU!
You are loved beyond compare.

From your glasses to your toenails
to your haircut to your skin,
the way you go from here to there—
you're one FANTASTIC kid.

So if you're feeling nervous
to talk to someone new,
just remember that's okay.
WE'VE ALL FELT THIS WAY TOO.

No matter where you go,
you've got what it takes.
Be exactly **WHO YOU ARE**.
You were made without mistakes.

So keep these ideas with you
when the lonelies make you blue.
It's true, YOU'LL ALWAYS HAVE A FRIEND.

Just keep on being YOU.